THE ART OF THE

PRE-RAPHAELITES

Edmund Swinglehurst

A Compilation of Works from the
BRIDGEMAN ART LIBRARY

•PARRAGON•

Pre-Raphaelites

This edition first published in Great Britain in 1994
by Parragon Book Service Limited

© 1994 Parragon Book Service Limited

ISBN 1 85813 611 3

Printed in Italy

Editor: Alexa Stace
Designer: Robert Mathias

The publishers would like to thank Joanna Hartley
at the Bridgeman Art Library for her invaluable help

THE PRE-RAPHAELITES

THE PRE-RAPHAELITE BROTHERHOOD, identified in its earliest work by the mysterious initials, PRB, was an association of painters, formed in London in 1848. Its chief members were William Holman Hunt, John Everett Millais and Dante Gabriel Rossetti, the oldest of whom, Hunt, was still only 21. As a group, the Brotherhood lasted for little more than a decade, but the impetus it gave to leading Victorian art in a new direction lasted until the early years of the 20th century.

Until the Brotherhood made its mark, British art was very much dominated by the Royal Academy, founded in the early years of George III's reign, and its first President, Joshua Reynolds. Despite the work of men such as Turner and Constable, the style of painting favoured by the Royal Academy tended towards that of the Old Masters, with copious use of brown paint. The three youthful Pre-Raphaelites deliberately challenged the established view of art, drawing up a manifesto of their intentions and publishing them in the four issues of a periodical called *The Germ*. They would paint direct from nature, with objective truthfulness and genuine ideas in sympathy with what was direct and heartfelt in the art of the past – particularly art before Raphael.

To emulate the work of the great Italian artists who had preceded Raphael, the painters of the Brotherhood made meticulous studies of the colours in nature, reproducing them brightly and clearly and working them into a wet, white ground. They went to inordinate lengths to find exact models for the settings and people in their pictures. In their desire to depict genuine, deeply significant themes they turned to the Bible for inspiration. Among the most significant of their early paintings were Hunt's *Light of the World* and *The Hireling Shepherd,* Millais' *Christ in the House of his Parents* and Rossetti's two versions of the Annunciation theme.

Initially, critics, including Charles Dickens, were hostile. They disliked the kind of realism that showed Christ's father as a working man with dirty fingernails and the Virgin as an ordinary young girl. The PRB was seen to be setting itself up as something better than Raphael; its members were also suspected of Romanist tendencies (this was the period of the Oxford Movement). But the great critic John Ruskin defended them strongly and the new painters soon had their admirers, particularly among the increasingly affluent middle classes of the Midlands and North of England.

The high-minded aims of the Brotherhood proved insufficient to hold the interest of Rossetti's fertile imagination and the restless skills of Millais for long. Only Hunt stayed faithful to the ideals of the Brotherhood. The other two developed in other directions, replacing biblical inspiration with that of the medieval world, the plays of Shakespeare and other sources made popular by the Romantic movement of the early 19th century.

Though the Brotherhood dissolved in about 1853, the new climate in art was one with which many other artists identified.

Foremost among them was Ford Madox Brown, a friend of the Brotherhood artists who shared their ideas. Brown, who had been born abroad and received his artistic training in Europe, was not much drawn to the biblical aspects of the Brotherhood's work and its close identification with the religious ethos of the time in England. His early paintings were more Romantic in character, often based on the poetry of Byron.

As Queen Victoria's reign lengthened, the British became more aware of their Imperial role. Interest grew in classical literature and the history of ancient Greece and Rome, as well as in the legendary medieval past of Britain itself. In art, Edward Burne-Jones was the prolific master of both the classical and the medieval scene, producing works like the *Pygmalion* series and *King Cophetua and the Beggarmaid* in

which the theme of the moral superiority of nobility of character above worldly wealth began to appear.

The classical theme, once established, provided a splendid opportunity for artists to combine sex and art in a tasteful manner acceptable to Victorian sensibility. Encouraged by the Royal Academy, artists produced more and more delectable paintings of Greek and Roman ladies at their bath and in other intimate situations. The technical standards of these paintings, set by the Pre-Raphaelites, were very high and were maintained throughout the period, for Victorian patrons would not accept anything other than expert craftsmanship.

Among the new generation of classical painters were men like Leighton (given a peerage), Poynter and Alma-Tadema (both knighted), whose idealized visions of the lives of ancient Greeks and Romans had the comfortable serenity of fairy tales.

There were other currents at work in the stream of art, an important one having been set in motion by Rossetti, who was a poet as well as a painter. He developed an idiosyncratic style full of mysterious undertones, using colour not to describe nature realistically but to suggest mood and feeling. This became the artistic theme which Walter Pater, an admirer of the Pre-Raphaelites, expressed in his writings on art, which were to stir up new ideas and attitudes. These ideas, though not to everyone's taste, represented a change in attitude prevalent in the more affluent society of the century's close, who saw in the cultured hedonism of such paintings as Godward's *Dolce Far Niente* or Solomon's *The Lovers* an acceptable philosophy of life.

Alongside this intimate boudoir art ran a continuing tendency to paint epic scenes. John Byam Shaw's *Love the Conqueror,* branded by one critic as trivial, was painted in 1899, when Impressionism, which had seized the high ground of art in France and was opening the gates to 20th-century painting, was already a generation old. In truth, Pre-Raphaelitism had had its day; although it hung on in British art until after World War I, it no longer represented the feelings and ideas of society.

△ **The Hireling Shepherd** 1851   William Holman Hunt (1827-1910)

Oil on canvas

WILLIAM HOLMAN HUNT was one of the founder members of the Pre-Raphaelite Brotherhood, with Dante Gabriel Rossetti and John Everett Millais. This painting was one of the first to incorporate the aims of the Brotherhood, which were to paint realistic and truthful paintings with a high moral tone. In search of a suitable background for *The Hireling* *Shepherd* Hunt went with his friend Millais to Ewell in Surrey. Having found what he wanted, he painted a detailed landscape in which he left a blank space for the figures, which he painted in later. The painting is full of the symbolism characteristic of Hunt's work. The shepherd, clearly a hireling, is evidently neglecting the sheep and is thus, by implication, not a 'good' shepherd. The small barrel of beer at his waist suggests a taste for pleasure above duty. The shepherdess, who is feeding green apples to a lamb, is also evidently careless of her responsibilities. This high-minded approach to art, perfectly in tune with public taste at the time, ensured the painting a good reception when it was exhibited at the Royal Academy.

▷ The Light of the World
1853   William Holman Hunt

Oil on canvas on panel

HUNT WROTE TO HIS FRIEND William Bell Scott to explain that in undertaking this subject he had felt impelled to do so by divine command. His original intention had been to make it a daytime scene, but he changed his mind at the idea of the challenge of a night picture, something he had never attempted before. As was his usual habit, Hunt set off with a friend, C.A. Collins, in search of a background. After walking with a lantern in the neighbourhood of Ewell station he found a workman's hut which he decided to use. He also found an orchard where he erected a straw hut from which he could study the effect of moonlight through the trees. For the face of Christ he created a composite of the faces of friends and 'departed heroes'. When first exhibited, the painting did not receive the acclaim that Hunt had hoped for. In the course of time, largely through the publication of engravings, it became one of the most potent icons of the 19th and early 20th centuries.

◁ **The Awakening Conscience**
1853   William Holman Hunt

Oil on canvas

THIS PAINTING is a perfect
example of Hunt's
preoccupation with finding
exactly the right setting for his
narrative. Although the exact
location of the room in this
painting has not been
identified, there is no doubt
that Hunt found a real room
that suited his purpose and
then filled it with the symbolic
matter that would point the
moral of his painting. The
expression in the young
woman's eyes as she draws
away from the man tells the
story well enough, but to make
sure that everyone
understands, Hunt has laid a
soiled glove on the carpet at
her feet and introduced a cat
from which a bird is trying to
escape. On the piano is a piece
of music entitled 'Oft in the
stilly night' and above it a
corner of a painting, *The
Woman Taken in Adultery*. The
young man at the piano

Detail

appears oblivious to the young
woman's awakening; so,
according to Ruskin, were the
public when the picture was
first shown. The critic of the
art magazine, *The Athenaeum*,
opined that many thought the
painting represented a quarrel
between brother and sister.

▷ **The Scapegoat** 1854-5
William Holman Hunt

Oil on canvas

VISITING THE HOLY LAND in 1854 in search of scenes to use in paintings of the life of Christ, Hunt hit on the idea for *The Scapegoat,* from the account in Leviticus of how, as part of the Jewish ritual of Atonement, two goats are selected, one to be sacrificed and the other to be released into the wilderness to atone for the sins of the community. The goat became, in Hunt's concept of the ritual, Jesus Christ himself, 'Despised and rejected of men . . .

. . . wounded for our transgressions'. Hunt found a goat, tethered it near the Dead Sea and studied and painted it for days on end. He made two versions of *The Scapegoat,* the first including a rainbow that appeared as he painted and the second, without the rainbow, of a goat with a white fleece, symbol of purity and lack of sin. In both versions he included the skull of an ibex, though in this version the skull and horns have become separated. The ibex skull was added to oblige a friend who had told Hunt that he should have used a goat with curved horns.

◁ The Lantern Maker's Courtship: a Street Scene in Cairo 1854
William Holman Hunt

Oil on canvas

HUNT VISITED CAIRO in 1854, before the opening of the Suez Canal made Egypt a tourist destination. He was much impressed by the, to him, alien culture and by the street life, which gave him the idea for this genre painting. Making a drawing of the shop where he had witnessed this scene, Hunt found himself up against the Islamic prohibition of the depiction of people. He finally found a young man prepared to pose but had to paint the girl from memory. In the background he included his friend Millais, arguing with shopkeepers, and a camel blocking the street. Owing to these and other difficulties, Hunt did not finish the painting in time to exhibit it at that year's Royal Academy show, though it was much admired by those he showed it to privately. Hunt later made another version of it.

▷ **The Lady of Shalott** 1886-1905   William Holman Hunt

Oil on canvas

HUNT FIRST BEGAN to work out ideas for a painting based on Tennyson's poem 'The Lady of Shalott' in 1850, but did not begin painting it until 1886. By this time the status of women in society had begun to change and the movement for women's emancipation was beginning to make itself heard. Perhaps it was this that made Hunt choose to paint the moment when the Lady of Shalott, condemned to see life only as a reflection in a mirror, decides to rebel and looks out of the window at Sir Lancelot. Her punishment for this will be death, though there is no hint of this in Hunt's painting, which he did not finish to exhibition standard until nearly 20 years after he started it. It has been called the last great Pre-Raphaelite painting and is indeed one of Hunt's finest works, its swirling lines making it a precursor of art nouveau.

◁ **Christ in the House of His Parents** 1850 John Everett Millais (1826-96)

Oil on canvas

THIS WAS MILLAIS'S first religious painting and was exhibited at the Royal Academy in 1850, where its realism caused a furore. The conservatism of academic paintings of the day, with their dark brown bitumen and idealized subjects, was what the Pre-Raphaelites had set out to defy, so the reaction to this picture could be seen as a good start for the Brotherhood. The public and art critics objected to the painting because it showed Christ's family as ordinary people, to the extent of depicting Joseph with dirty fingernails. Even Charles Dickens, tolerant about other matters, described the Christ child as 'a hideous, wry-necked, blubbering, red-haired boy in a night-gown'. The publicity excited by the painting provoked Queen Victoria into requesting a private viewing. Her opinion is not known, but Millais is quoted as saying that he hoped the painting 'would not have a bad effect on her mind'.

◁ **Waiting** 1854
John Everett Millais

Oil on panel

THIS SMALL PICTURE painted on
a panel was probably done in
springtime, to judge by the
vegetation. It has a freshness
of colour about it which is one
of the distinguishing features
of Millais' early work. It seems
to have been a study for a later
painting entitled *A Highland
Lassie,* for which the model was
Euphemia Chalmers Gray
whom Millais married in 1855.
It has also been suggested that
the model for the waiting
woman was Holman Hunt's
girlfriend but there is no proof
of this other than that Hunt
and Millais were close friends.
The painting has the air of a
moment in time seized and
recorded, much as the
Impressionists were to do later
in the century.

▷ **Autumn Leaves** 1855-56
John Everett Millais

Oil on canvas

WRITING TO AN AMERICAN
reviewer of this painting,
Millais agreed that it was not
intended to be a narrative
picture but one of mood. 'I
intended the picture to
awaken by its solemnity the
deepest religious reflection', he
wrote. The setting is the
garden of the Millais home,
Annat Lodge, in Perth,
Scotland, and the girls
burning leaves are Alice, sister
of Millais's wife, Effie, (in the
centre) and friends. Effie
described the painting of the
picture and the patience of the
models in some detail and
reported Millais's words, 'He
never had such good models.
When they were not wanted
they sat in the kitchen, helped
to peel potatoes or watched
the door or sat still looking
into the fire for hours in
perfect idleness, quite happy.'
Millais sold the painting to
James Eden, a collector who
owned a bleaching works , for
£700; Eden later exchanged it
with another collector.

Detail

▷ **Trust Me**   John Everett Millais

Oil on canvas

THE PRE-RAPHAELITES' concern for moral values and social behaviour derived from the new society that was being created in Britain as a result of the Industrial Revolution, along with the first questionings of old-established values. The resulting conflict was a subject that interested the Pre-Raphaelite painters. In this picture, Millais records what was perhaps a not unfamiliar situation in a middle-class household such as his own: a father demands to see the letter that has arrived in the postbag he is holding and his daughter is reluctant to show what she considers to be her private correspondence.

▷ **Ophelia** 1852 John Everett Millais

Oil on canvas

Ophelia was painted at about the same time as Holman Hunt's *Hireling Shepherd*. Millais found the stream that provided the setting for his painting near Ewell, where Hunt had also found settings for his pictures. Millais' painting is full of Shakespearean allusions: the rose in the dead Ophelia's hand is a reference to her brother Laertes's description of her as 'the Rose of May' and the robin in the undergrowth is a reminder of Ophelia's song 'For bonny sweet robin is all my joy'. A true Pre-Raphaelite, Millais spent a great deal of time on the exact reproduction of the stream and the overhanging trees. Despite his care, after it was exhibited (it was hung next to Hunt's *Hireling Shepherd*) the painting's colour deteriorated and Millais was obliged to retouch it. The model was Elizabeth Siddal, later Rossetti's wife. Millais made her pose fully dressed in a bathtub, as a result of which she, not surprisingly, caught cold.

▷ **Sir Isumbras at the Ford: A Dream of the Past** 1857
John Everett Millais

Oil on canvas

THE KINDLY OLD KNIGHT and trusting children represent a Victorian view of the relationship between the old and young and was no doubt painted, like much of Millais's later work, with an eye on public sentiment. The legendary Sir Isumbras was a haughty lord who became more tolerant and soft-hearted after a series of misfortunes came his way. Millais evidently had high hopes for this work; when it did not find a buyer at the Royal Academy Exhibition of 1857, where it was criticized by Ruskin, he took it back to his studio and kicked a hole in it. In fact, Millais was not really happy with his treatment of the horse, which had come out larger than he intended. The size of the horse so worried Millais that he asked his friend, Tom Taylor, a journalist,to write a stanza justifying the horse's size.

◁ **The Boyhood of Raleigh** 1870   John Everett Millais

Oil on canvas

CHEAPLY AVAILABLE PRINTS of this painting hung in nearly every schoolroom in Britain for decades, its inspirational character reminding everyone of Britain's hard-won role as the mistress of the world's oceans. By the time Millais painted this work, he was well settled in his marriage to Effie, former wife of John Ruskin, and he himself was a well-regarded member of the artistic establishment, having been elected RA in 1863. From this period, his style became looser and his subjects more popular in character. Less uncompromising than Hunt, Millais became more sentimental as he grew older and completed his life's work with such paintings as *Cherry Ripe* and *Bubbles* which, though immensely popular among the public, did little to enhance his artistic reputation.

◁ **The Annunciation:
Ecce Ancilla Domini** 1850
Dante Gabriel Rossetti
(1828-82)

Oil on canvas

ROSSETTI EXHIBITED this
painting at the Royal Academy
in 1850, when Hunt showed
his *Early Britons Sheltering a
Missionary from the Druids* and
Millais his *Christ in the House of
His Parents* (page 17). All three
treated Christian subjects in
accordance with the beliefs of
their Pre-Raphaelite
Brotherhood, formed just two
years previously. In painting
this Annunciation in such a
realistic manner Rossetti was
breaking with tradition. Italian
Renaissance artists showed the
Virgin as a holy figure, isolated
from everyday life by her
situation. Rossetti's Virgin is an
ordinary girl, bewildered and
frightened by the news that
the angel has just given her.
This unorthodox approach,
which enraged large sections
of the art-loving public, was in
keeping with the Pre-
Raphaelite commitment to
paint truthfully.

▷ **The Annunciation** 1855
Dante Gabriel Rossetti

Watercolour

THIS IS A VERY different
Annunciation from the one
subtitled *Ecce Ancilla Domini*
(page 28). The figure of the
Virgin was based on a drawing
of Elizabeth Siddal which
Rossetti had done in 1854.
Siddal had been discovered by
Deverell, a friend of the Pre-
Raphaelites, working as a sales
girl and he introduced her to
the group who used her as a
model. From about 1852 she
modelled only for Rossetti and
the two were married in 1860.
Two years later, she was found
dying from an overdose of
laudanum, taken in a
depressed state after the death
of her newborn daughter. In
this Annunciation Rossetti has
adopted a freer brushwork
than in the earlier one, though
he is still using a Pre-
Raphaelite symbolism: the
Virgin is raising a cupped
hand of water, symbol of
purity, as the dove hovers over
her. The watercolour was one
of a series of scenes from the
life of the Virgin which
Rossetti worked on
throughout the 1850s.

◁ **The Beloved (The Bride)**
1865-6
Dante Gabriel Rossetti

Oil on canvas

IN ROSSETTI'S WORK the
religious idealism of the early
Pre-Raphaelite Brotherhood
gradually gave way to a new
kind of spirituality in which
sensuality was a heady
ingredient. In this painting the
biblical reference is to the
Song of Solomon: 'My beloved
is mine and I am his. Let him
kiss me with the kisses of his
mouth: for thy love is better
than wine'. The Victorian
inclination to conceal real
motives for their actions led
F. G. Stephens to describe this
painting as an expression of
'the power of women to move
men'. The model for the
young woman, showing herself
to her betrothed surrounded
by her friends and a young
black girl, was a girl called
Maria Ford.

May Morris 1872
Dante Gabriel Rossetti

Coloured chalks

▷ *Overleaf, page 32*

MAY MORRIS was one of the
two daughters of the poet and
craftsman, William Morris and
his wife Jane. In this beautiful
study, Rossetti has given May a
strong look of her mother,
with whom Rossetti was
infatuated, although there was
no question of intimacy
between them. Almost every
woman he painted had
something of Jane about her.
This painting bears the
inscription 'M.M. aetat X1872',
the year of Rossetti's
schizophrenic collapse. Both
May and her sister Jenny were
fond of Rossetti, who often
asked after them. On one such
occasion Jane replied, rather
strangely, that May was a
delicate child and would not
drag through a long life. 'So
much the better for her'. In
fact, May lived well into the
20th century, quite long
enough to edit her father's
works and to write a biography
of him.

◁ **The Lady of Pity** c 1875
Dante Gabriel Rossetti

Oil on canvas

The Lady of Pity is a typically romantic view of Jane Morris as Rossetti saw her, with her grey eyes, full lips and abundant hair all emphasized. Rossetti found the combination of sensuality and intellectuality in Jane tantalizing and he had a close but not physical relationship with the wife of his friend William Morris. In the scroll under the portrait Rossetti, who was of Italian origin, has written 'color d'amore e di pietà sembiante' (the colour of love and appearance of pity). Rossetti's Italian Romanticism aroused some criticism. A reviewer in the *Contemporary Review* in 1871 referred to Rossetti's poetry as 'The fleshly school of poetry, never spiritual, never tender, always self-conscious and aesthetic . . . a stupendous preponderance of sensibility and sickly animalism'. This greatly upset Rossetti ,who soon after suffered a schizophrenic breakdown.

▷ **Astarte Syriaca** 1877
Dante Gabriel Rossetti

Oil on canvas

ASTARTE, the Syrian goddess of
love, was both caring and
cruel. By using Jane Morris as
the model for her Rossetti was
perhaps saying something
about his inner torments
concerning Jane. Perhaps, too,
he was saying something about
the theme of unrequited love,
which had a great vogue in
Victorian times. Other heroes
and heroines admired for their
abnegation included Dante
and Beatrice and Petrarch and
Laura, who also featured in
the Victorian iconography of
love. During the hours she
spent posing for this painting
Jane discovered how much
Rossetti was addicted to the
drug chloral and this, as well
as her awareness of his
obsession with her, may have
decided her to distance herself
a little from the artist.

◁ **The Day-dream** 1880
Dante Gabriel Rossetti

Oil on canvas

ROSSETTI PAINTED this splendid
work after Jane Morris had
ceased to pose regularly for
him; it was done from an
earlier drawing of Jane sitting
in a tree at Kelmscott, the
home that Rossetti shared with
the Morrises on the Thames.
The book she is holding is a
reference to her love of
reading and the sycamore tree
with its unfolding buds is a
symbol of spring. The spray of
honeysuckle in Jane's hand is
also a symbol, its heady scent
and tongue-like petals
suggesting the sexual love that
Rosetti felt for her but which
could never be satisfied. When
this picture was painted
Rossetti had abandoned the
Pre-Raphaelite principles of
his early years and his
aesthetic art style was well
developed.

▷ **Manfred on the Jungfrau**
1842
Ford Madox Brown (1821-93)

Oil on canvas

FORD MADDOX BROWN's birth
in France and 10 years of
study as an artist in Bruges
and Antwerp predisposed him
to Romantic subjects in the
style of Delacroix, though his
admiration for the Romantics
was tempered by his
admiration for the
draughtsmanship of David, the
classical painter of Napoleonic
France. This early painting,
based on a poem by that most
romantic of English poets,
Lord Byron, shows the two
tendencies combining in
Brown's work. He has chosen
to depict the moment in
Byron's poem, 'Manfred',
when the hero is about to leap
off the mountain to his
death.The expression on the
face is frozen in a dramatic
grimace and the body
language is derived from
French rhetorical paintings.
The painting was actually
completed in Paris about 1842,
a year after he had conceived
the composition in Brussels.

▷ **Stages of Cruelty** 1856-90   Ford Madox Brown

Oil on canvas

ALTHOUGH FORD MADOX BROWN was never a member of the Pre-Raphaelite Brotherhood, he felt great sympathy for their aims and ideas. Before returning to England in the late 1840s, he had picked up ideas similar to the Pre-Raphaelites from the Nazarenes, a German-based group of painters who admired mediaeval themes and style and painted in bright clear colours. Brown met Rossetti after his Continental studies and was so impressed by his work that he asked to receive lessons from him. Brown shared the Pre-Raphaelite taste for everyday subjects with moral implications and symbolic meanings. In this painting he uses the lovers for his narrative and makes his symbolic points with the convolvulus, signifying entanglements, climbing up the steps. The small girl about to hit the dog reflects the often unthinking nature of cruelty. Brown had some difficulty in completing the painting because the models for the lovers were unreliable and also because no one showed any interest in commissioning it. He eventually sold it in 1887.

△ **Work** 1852-65   Ford Madox Brown

Oil on canvas

IN *Work*, painted partly in the open air in Heath Street, Hampstead, he shows the various categories of work, from manual labour to intellectual work (symbolized by Carlyle and F. D. Maurice on the right of the picture). Brown had spent two years as a teacher in Maurice's Working Men's College. The painting was made on a white ground, rather than the brown currently used, in order to enhance the colour. The painting was almost completed when a potential buyer, a Mr Plint, insisted that it lacked moral and religious significance and obliged Brown to add a lady distributing tracts (on the left). Unfortunately, Plint died before Brown finished his work, but when it was exhibited in 1865 Plint's estate bought it.

▷ **The Last Of England**
1852-55   Ford Madox Brown

Oil on panel

THE POIGNANCY of this picture of unhappy emigrants must have struck a chord in many hearts at a time when many Britons were being forced to emigrate in search of a better life. Perhaps Brown's own situation as a struggling and impecunious artist contributed to his depiction of the sad desperation of the couple in this famous painting. He himself had reached the point of considering whether to emigrate to India but was saved by the sale of this painting. The ship on which the couple and their child are leaving is evidently on a long voyage, for fresh vegetables have been tied along the rails and in the background is a lifeboat also full of provisions – a cabin boy is selecting some for the first meal aboard.

◁ She Shall Be Called Woman

1892-93   George Frederick
Watts (1817-1904)

Oil on canvas

WATTS WAS A TALENTED young
man who first exhibited at the
Royal Academy at the age of
20 and later won a prize in a
competition for the decoration
of the Houses of Parliament.
The money enabled him to go
to Italy where he studied the
Renaissance painters. On his
return to England he became a
successful portraitist and a
painter of allegorical scenes
which the public associated
with the highest form of art.
She Shall Be Called Woman is a
typical Watts female nude with
a high-sounding title. His
technique was very individual
for he did not like the glossy
finish of most contemporary
oil paintings and would put his
colours on blotting paper to
diminish their oil content. He
also had a freer style than such
contemporaries as Leighton
and Alma-Tadema. Watts'
declared aims were to paint
pictures that appealed 'to the
intellect and refined emotions
rather than the senses.'

▷ **Hope** 1885   George Frederick Watts

Oil on canvas

IN THIS PAINTING of a blindfolded woman with a broken lyre Watts was expressing the sentiments of such popular aphorisms as 'Never despair' or 'Where there is life there is hope', though his painting seems to be suggesting the opposite. The Victorian public understood his message, however, and the painting became enormously popular, especially after it was reproduced as an engraving. Watts's talents extended into other branches of the arts; he was a fresco painter and sculptor (one of his statues, *Physical Energy*, is in Kensington Gardens in London). Offered a baronetcy for his contribution to art, Watts refused, though he later accepted the Order of Merit. The best of his work was undoubtedly his portraiture, including studies of Carlyle and Tennyson, which showed a depth of understanding of his subjects' characters.

▷ **Love and the Maiden**
John Roddam Spencer Stanhope (1829-1908)

Oil on canvas

THE INFLUENCE of Spencer Stanhope's lifelong friend Burne-Jones is clearly visible in this painting, in which the god of love approaches a young woman in a wood by the edge of the sea. The painted flowers are typical of the precise Pre-Raphaelite technique in which every inch of the painting is in focus.

The theme belongs to the aesthetic period of paintings of which Rossetti was a protagonist and which nurtured the seeds of art for art's sake, propounded by Walter Pater, friend of the Pre-Raphaelites, whose concepts were criticized for being an encouragement to cultural hedonism.

◁ **Washing Day** John Roddam Spencer Stanhope

SPENCER STANHOPE came from an affluent middle-class family and was educated at Rugby and Christchurch, Oxford. He began to study art with G. F. Watts in 1850, visiting Italy with him in 1853. He became one of the circle of young artists around the Pre-Raphaelites in the mid-1850s and was particularly friendly with Burne-Jones, who influenced his painting and became a lifelong friend. He first exhibited at the Royal Academy in 1859 and later at the Grosvenor Gallery. Like his artist friends, he had a sympathy for ordinary people and often chose subjects showing them at work, though often in an idealized manner. *Washing Day* in which the women wash the clothes while the men get on with the business of fishing, is typical of Stanhope's work.

▷ **Winding the Skein** 1878
Frederic Leighton (1830-96)

Oil on canvas

LEIGHTON, who became the only British artist to be made a peer, had a privileged upbringing thanks to his father, a Scarborough doctor. He ensured that his son was given a thorough classical education and also learnt French, German and Italian, thus gaining some first-hand experience of European culture. This background, and his sociable manner and good looks, ensured Leighton a comfortable place in British society. After he was 25 Leighton's work became more and more influenced by Hellenistic culture which he considered 'the most perfect balance of transcendent gifts' The setting for *Winding the Skein,* a Roman or Greek house with a terrace looking out to sea, suggests the calm, contemplative life which Leighton ascribed to Greek culture, though its very perfection gives it a bland character which subsequent generations have found soporific.